OUTLINING

How to structure examinations in civil litigation

JOHN HOLLANDER

A PUBLICATION OF

EST. 2007

ADVOCACY CLUB BOOKS

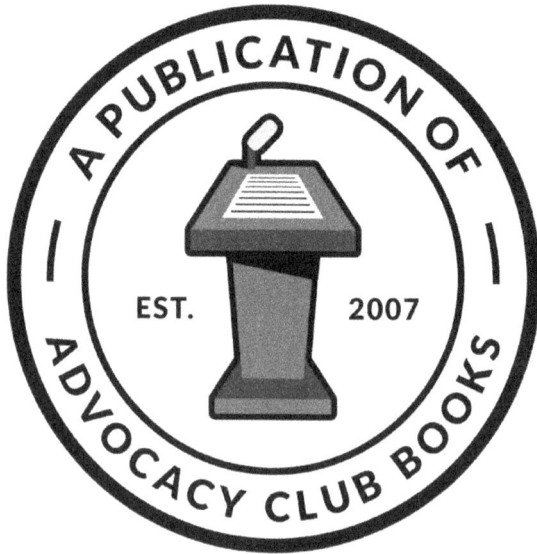

ISBN 0995991006

ISBN 9780995991002 (paperback)

THE ADVOCACY CLUB BOOKS SERIES

Introduction to Trial Advocacy: *How Canadian lawyers prepare for and conduct civil cases*

Outlining: *How to structure examinations in civil litigation*

Estate Litigation: *Trial advocacy techniques in Canadian estate cases*

COPYRIGHT NOTICE

Outlining: How to structure examinations in civil cases

Copyright © John Hollander, 2015

Published in 2017 by John Hollander Professional Corporation, #500-265 Carling Avenue, Ottawa, Ontario, Canada K1S 2E1

ISBN 0995991006

ISBN 9780995991002 (paperback)

TABLE OF CONTENTS

OUTLINING

CHAPTER 1: CASE ANALYSIS: IT'S ALL ABOUT CONTEXT

- *This chapter reacquaints the reader with the principles of case analysis.*

- *It then applies those principles to the case study, step by step.*

An examination is a wasted opportunity unless it is the application of case analysis. As Yogi Berra famously put it, "if you don't know where you're going, you might end up someplace else." This brings us to context. What is the perfect question for a specific situation? That depends on many factors:

- What are the goals for the examination?

- What is the best sequence of questions to attain those goals?

- Within that sequence, where does the question fit?

- What reaction is likely from the witness?

- What will you ask if the answer deviates from the one expected?

- What will you do next?

CASE ANALYSIS REVISITED

There is not sufficient space to rehash the technique for case analysis. This was thoroughly laid out in the Young

Advocates Series (YAS) handbook, *Case Analysis - the critical path to persuasion*. A summary also appears in a chapter in the initial handbook in this series, *Introduction to Trial Advocacy*.

The formula for case analysis applies to the facts and issues in any case, such as the case study. With that in mind, this chapter will do just that. It applies the principles to the facts of the case study.

It may be helpful to revisit the introductory handbook so that the principles are fresh in your mind. Before you read the next couple of pages, try to work out the steps of case analysis by yourself.

- Start with the neutral facts. Identify the essential ones. Eliminate the others, at least for now.

- Then, proceed to identify the issue. Spin the issue as best reflects the interests of each of the parties.

- Then apply the new themes to the elements for one side and then for the other.

- Consider the back story. What other factors may move an observer to prefer one side over the other?

It is essential that you choose a side before you start the process. Plaintiff or Defence? The two sides do not agree on spin, but they agree on several elements. As is often said, people are entitled to their opinions, but facts are facts.

At this point, please consult the case study at the back of this handbook. It introduces the characters, the deceased,

Brian, his nieces - the sisters, Louise (estranged) and Carol (actively involved), and the lawyers, Lee (partner) and Kim (junior associate). The case study contains a case summary, a timeline, witness statements from the four living witnesses/participants and a few exhibits.

When reviewing the witness statements and exhibits, start to develop arguments that fit the facts. For example, Kim's inexperience is a fact. Is it helpful or harmful to your position? Why? How might you exploit this?

As another example, it is unlikely that Louise has much to say about this issue (in her capacity as a witness), but what about the other witnesses? How will Kim's youth play to the audience as part of the back story?

What other arguments occur to you? Case analysis identifies the points necessary to make your case and break theirs. The arguments pro and con then flow from those points. As lawyers work on their cases, the points and arguments develop over time. This is not a law school exercise, where all the facts are presented in one batch (like is our case study).

The process is similar to the writing exercise of the journalist or historian. Ideally, they start with the neutral facts. They work these facts to generate arguments that highlight the significance of some of those facts, but not of others. This "work" creates the spin that leads to the conclusion the writer intends, the thesis of the article, essay or book.

Lawyers start with their client's interest as their point of view. Writers may not have that starting point. Once in motion, however, the process of case analysis is the same in each of these pursuits.

ANALYSIS OF THE CASE STUDY

Step one, identify the facts. In this step, we sift through all of the facts in the witness statements and the exhibits to glean just those facts that connect the dots between the duty of care and the damages.

- Brian has two nieces, Carol and Louise.

- Brian makes a will leaving his estate to Carol.

- Brian gets very sick, is confined to hospital.

- Brian, through Carol, contacts his lawyer to change his will.

- Kim visits Brian to take instructions to change the will to give 50% to Louise.

- Brian dies three weeks later, without Kim having done the will.

- Louise misses out on $200,000 of inheritance.

Step two, identify the issue. In this step, we establish what it is the court will be asked to decide (if it gets to court).

- Whether Kim's failure to implement Brian's wishes breached her duty of care owed to Louise.

Step three, spin the issue. In this step, we try to establish how each of the parties will try to characterize the issue.

- For Louise, whether Lee assigned a rookie to perform a professional's task, thereby jeopardizing the rights of Louise. The sales pitch might be: All it took was a handwritten codicil. How hard could that be? Risk of early death was high. The professional has to take this into account.

- For Kim and Lee, whether their compliance with their client's direct instructions is actionable. The sales pitch might be: The client knows best and gave instructions here. If the client is incapable of giving instructions, then the new will would not be valid. It's not about what Kim wanted. It's all about what Brian directed. And who knows what Brian would have done in an office with proper advice?

Step four, spin the elements for Louise. In this step, we review each of the elements and recast them in a way that favors the interests of the client.

- Brian has two nieces, his favorite, Carol, and the estranged Louise.

- Brian makes a will leaving his estate to Carol.

- Brian gets very sick, confined to hospital, facing his mortality.

- Brian has his wits about him. The law presumes this to be true.

- Brian reconciles with Louise and wants to make things right by redoing his will.

- Lee assigns the inexperienced Kim to take instructions, which are to change the will to allocate his estate equally between his beloved nieces.

- Brian dies three weeks later, with Lee and Associates doing nothing at all to prepare the will.

- Louise misses out on what is rightfully hers.

Step five, spin the elements for the opposition. In this step, we recast the elements in a way that we expect the opposition to try to accomplish.

- Brian makes a will leaving his estate to his niece, Carol.

- Brian gets very sick, confined to hospital.

- Brian contacts his lawyer to redo his will.

- Lee and Associates send Kim to meet Brian.

- Due to site conditions in the hospital, Kim cannot perform proper capacity assessment or conduct a proper will intake interview. There is therefore no retainer and no will instruction.

- Kim receives instructions to wait until Brian is discharged from hospital, with his capacity to give this direction presumed by law.

- Brian dies three weeks later, without being discharged or changing his instructions.

- Carol receives what is rightfully hers, compliant with the written directions of Brian and his only valid will.

With the above exercise in mind, we are now able to anticipate what each side will try to accomplish with each step in the litigation. Until we perform this analysis, how could we know what to ask, and in what order?

It seems the real issue may be whether Kim should have explained the risks to Brian and taken any of these steps to mitigate them:

- Draft the will right away and return to hospital, that day or next.

- Holographic will in a hospital, dictated by Kim.

- Codicil in hospital, written by Kim.

CHAPTER 2: THE OUTLINE: WHAT DOES IT LOOK LIKE? PART 1

- *This chapter introduces the format for the examination outline.*

- *Identifies several objectives and attributes for the successful outline.*

- *Suggests methods to adapt the outline to suit the individual examiner.*

While formulae make sense in litigation, one size rarely fits all. Consider how much of a prompt a novice lawyer requires, compared to a senior litigator. As an exercise, ask a senior litigator to show you the outline used in a recent deposition, direct or cross-examination. Odds are that it differs dramatically from something that you would be able to use in a similar situation.

WHY BOTHER?

One consideration is just why a lawyer needs an outline in the first place. The outline serves as a roadmap that identifies each of the subjects that the lawyer has to explore. The purpose of each point recorded in the outline is to prompt the lawyer to ask the next question correctly. That is really two purposes that serve to dictate the amount of detail required.

- The first purpose of the outline is to identify the questions.

- The second purpose is to phrase them well.

An experienced litigator may not require much in the way of a prompt for either of the two purposes. On the other hand, an inexperienced one may require the safety blanket of both.

HOW MUCH DETAIL?

This brings us to the amount of detail the lawyer requires in the outline. The purpose of the outline is to prompt the lawyer, like a cue given to a stage actor. The more complex the case and the greater the involvement of the witness, the greater the need for prompts. How many of these are necessary, and in what detail?

Consider the following, each of which will be dealt with in further detail below and in the next chapter.

- Headings and headlines, how to label (written) and then how to introduce (oral) each sequence of related questions.

- Specific points that the examiner wants to cover within a sequence.

- Specific language that might be significant to the case or to the point, either to stay within the theme or to adopt a technical standard.

- Sufficient detail of the points to allow the examiner to ask the questions.

- Tactical decisions that arise during any examination. Often, counsel can anticipate these.

- Sequence of headings, or of subheadings, like chapters and numbered paragraphs in a textbook.

- Incorporation of transcript, statement or exhibit references.

HEADLINES AND HEADINGS

Each outline should contain a label for the subjects covered. Each heading should suggest a headline that counsel will speak. I.e., the outline should serve as a prompt for the examiner to introduce the next subject to the witness (and the court, if at trial). This allows people to keep track of where the examiner is going. The subject of headlines is dealt with in much greater length in two of the handbooks in the Young Advocates Series, published by Irwin Law, on the subjects of *Discovery Techniques* and *Examinations*.

- A heading is the word or two that starts a sequence of points in an outline. For example, "Meeting, January 11."

- A headline is an oral statement used by counsel to introduce a subject. For example, "I will ask some questions about the meeting of January 11."

- In most cases, the heading or subheading suggests the headline that counsel will use during the examination.

Consider the heading to be the first level of the outline. In a tort case, there would be several headings for each chapter of the theory of the case: back story (who are the parties and how do they fit into the case), duty, breach of duty, causation, damages and often contributory negligence. It is not necessary to recite out loud that the subject is turning to liability. It is helpful to say out loud that the subject is turning to the events of a specific date. This might be the first sequence of questions about liability.

It is likely that the outline will contain a separate heading for each of the relevant events and subjects. Damages, for instance, could be broken into loss of general damages, loss of income, out-of-pocket expenses, etc. Each of these subjects warrants several more headings or subheadings.

Compare this process to that of a newspaper. There are several sections, such as World News, Local News, Sports, Business, Entertainment and the like. There are articles within each section, each with its own headline. These headlines serve the same purpose as the headlines in an examination outline. Unlike the newspaper situation, the headline should always be neutral. They should never indicate the slant of the questions. Headlines should not use evocative language, descriptive words and certainly not sarcasm or irony. For example, in the examination for discovery of Kim:

Correct: "I will now ask some questions about your meeting with Lee on January 12."

Incorrect: "I will now ask you about how Lee failed to tell you to do the will right away."

Headlines should be noncontroversial. An experienced litigator needs little in the way of a prompt to introduce the subject. An inexperienced one, on the other hand, might have to write out the full headline. This allows the lawyer to raise the subject adequately and without controversy.

SPECIFIC POINTS THAT THE EXAMINER WANTS TO COVER WITHIN A HEADLINE

As canvassed at greater length in the other two handbooks, each heading (headline) should be followed by a sequence of a few points. These should be tied together by the subject introduced by the headline.

An example of this sequence of headline followed by questions might an important meeting

Heading: meeting January 12

Headline: we will now discuss the meeting with Lee on January 12. The headline is then followed by a few targeted questions with respect to the meeting.

- How long was it?

- Where did it occur?

- Who attended?

- What was its purpose?

- What topics were discussed?

The headlines can also serve as a cluster of sub-headlines. Each of these would be, in effect, another headline. For example, "how long was it?" can become

Heading: duration

Headline: let's discuss how long the meeting lasted

- When start?

- When finished?

- How do you know?

- Notes made regarding the time?

The details of the points within the headline will be explored below.

Headlines should be noncontroversial. The topic heading, "the meeting" could be fleshed out into "let's talk about the meeting that occurred on that day." A descriptive word, such as "important" could be controversial. How important the meeting was might be quite different as between the parties to the lawsuit. The word should not be used if that is the case.

How much detail does the examiner require to ask the question in that manner? This is usually a function of the experience of the examiner. Sometimes the lawyer creating an outline is not the lawyer asking the questions. In that case, more detail is usually required to ensure that the examiner understands the purpose of the question.

SPECIFIC LANGUAGE

There may be an important word, concept or theme that counsel wants to adopt as part of the examination. It may be that the examiner wants to stress some specific, forceful and evocative language. The classic example of "crash" instead of "incident" applies here. Experienced lawyers do not require this level of prompting.

In a case involving technical concepts and case-specific language, the outline might use the precise word or phrase. In some cases it is preferable to use the same language to express a concept, with repetition supporting the theme.

Where the witness is an expert, the outline might contain a reminder of the technical language used by the expert (or by another expert). Again, the purpose is to keep the lawyer on track.

EXAMPLE FROM THE CASE STUDY

Before we give the proposed answer, try to create an outline that would permit you to examine Kim in a direct examination with respect to the meeting between Kim and Lee the day after the interview with Brian in the hospital, January 12.

Create a heading, headline and several points to be covered within the headline that together will cover the subject.

In the outline that follows, the words "broad to narrow" suggest a wide, open question. If the witness (Kim) misses any of the points that follow, these should be covered with follow-up questions. As such, the outline represents a checklist of points that the witness should cover before leaving the topic.

Heading: meeting, January 12

Headline: I will ask some questions about your meeting with Lee on January 12

- Tell us what happened (broad to narrow)

- Who arranged it

- What discussed

- POA

- Health or mortality of Brian

- Time to prepare will

- Help drafting will

- Lee's advice

- What was to happen next

CHAPTER 3: OUTLINING DETAIL, PART 2

- *The outline is a roadmap*

- *Details and levels depend on the examiner*

- *Each block, whether heading or subheading, should be portable in case the real-time situation warrants*

NESTED HEADINGS

Not everyone thinks in a linear manner. Examinations, however, must be linear. The examiner can only ask one question at a time. Examiners will confuse both their witnesses and the court with questions that circle back to topics already covered, or that wander aimlessly.

The outline's headings and subheadings should therefore identify and deal with the subjects in a logical, linear path. Introduce a subject. Complete the subject. Introduce the next one.

Some subjects require several subheadings. For example, the examination will cover a series of events. Many events may be related to the same subject. The heading may be the umbrella description of the subject. Each event then warrants a subheading of its own. It is the subheadings that get their own headlines. The witness gets no benefit from learning that the events relate to liability, or to duty, or to breach or whatever. The judge will figure this out, easily enough.

"Nesting" refers to the inclusion of subheadings within a heading. Of course, subheadings can themselves have subheadings. For example, consider this set of headlines for Lee's deposition, direct or cross-examination:

- "We can now turn to the events of January 11. First, I understand there was a call to your office." This introduces the sequence of questions about Carol's call.

- "Let's now turn to the meeting with Carol in the lobby." This introduces that sequence of questions.

- "And I will now ask about the meeting with Brian." And so on.

DETAILS OF THE POINTS

Each subheading in the outline will contain a list of the questions to be asked, and possibly a series of subheadings. Ideally, there should only be a few questions (or points) after each subheading. The number depends on the subject. For any practitioner, it might vary for depositions, directs and cross-examinations. The ideal is just a few, perhaps five or so. The reason is to ensure that both the witness and court connect the questions to the topic's headline.

An experienced litigator may only require the subheading. This suggests the headline. Perhaps a word or two to prompt for the point being sought. Less experienced counsel may require not only the subheading, but the headline and each of the important points within the headline.

TACTICAL DECISIONS

It is absolutely not the case that lawyers should only ask questions to which they know the answers. That happens only in dreams. Lawyers can, however, minimize these adventures into the unknown. They should predict when either the witness is most likely to go off script. Is the risk worth the reward? If there are two possible answers, as with a closed question, is one helpful and the other harmless? Consider alternate approaches.

This suggests a challenge facing bridge players. Let's say that the king and jack of trumps are in a closed hand to player's left. The player leads a small trump card from dummy and puts the queen on the table, not the ace. The player hopes that the hand to the right holds the king. The play is called a "finesse". Was there another way to play the cards that would avoid loss of the trick? Maybe the king was a singleton and the ace would drop it? Maybe another play forces the right hand to lead away from the king-jack into the player's ace-queen?

This illustrates the examiner's situation.

- In direct examinations, the examiner can prepare in advance. If something novel arises, the examiner probably can intuit the right decision from known facts.

- In discovery, the stakes are not so high, as the examiner may choose not to use the answer later.

- In cross, however, the gamble is immediate. The outline should anticipate these gambles and prompt the examiner to make the best choices.

It is possible that the lawyer cannot predict how a witness or court will react to a particular series of points. This is the moment for the lawyer to record an outline sequence that covers the different options: if this series works, then go to this next area. That is Plan A. If it fails to accomplish its objective, then try Plan B.

An example of Plan B thinking is the tactic of creeping up on a point. Consider this sequence of questions in a cross-examination of Carol about Louise' visits to Brian.

Heading: Louise and Brian

Headline: let's talk about your sister's visits with your uncle in the year before he went to City Hospital.

- She did visit

- Occasional

- Rare

- Hardly ever

- Maybe once

- Never

This sequence runs its course all the way to the unspoken punchline, which is "Louise had no relationship with her uncle." The purpose is to support a "gold-digging" theme.

If the answer to one of the questions is not helpful, counsel can cut it short and move to another headline and sequence. This is Plan B.

It is no coincidence that this is starting to resemble the battle plans of a military commander. Like the military analogy, however, plans often fall apart during implementation.

SEQUENCE OF HEADLINE POINTS

There are several benefits to the use of headlines during examinations. One of these is that the outline can consist of several movable subjects.

Consider as an example a series of headings in sequence to proceed from the identification of the witness, to creation of the duty of care, to breach of that duty. During the course of the examination, the lawyer determines that more testimony is required in a particular area. That part of the outline can be expanded or re-situated as the situation warrants.

There is no need to use all of the subject areas that counsel has identified in the outline. If there has been a stipulation made during the course of the examination, for example, the sequence becomes unnecessary. Similarly, there may be a great benefit to pursuing a point past its predicted endpoint if the lawyer is making effective headway. These are the judgment calls and tactical decisions that trial counsel have to make whenever they are on their feet.

The senior litigator requires very little prompting to ask all the questions to accomplish the objectives. Junior counsel may require far more in the way of detail. In the case of the experienced lawyer, training and experience fill in all the missing points.

This resembles the difference between head notes (great detail) and flash notes (little detail) of reported court decisions. The outline required by senior counsel usually does not contain full, grammatical sentences or questions. If the lawyer is worried about the exact phrasing of a question, the full question could appear in the outline. The inexperienced litigator requires more detail to be effective.

INCORPORATION OF TRANSCRIPT, STATEMENT OR EXHIBIT REFERENCES

Here is a major technique all counsel should adopt in their outline practice. They should refer to the documents (exhibits), witness statements and transcripts. We will call any of these items the "Material". References should include the exact location of both the Material and the relevant point in the Material. Early in the litigation, there may be a few documents and willsays. As trial approaches, files grow dramatically. At trial, counsel often bring bankers' boxes chock full of Material.

In direct examinations, counsel should be ready to present documents for identification as exhibits. In cross, they should ready to confront the witness with the witness' inconsistency with anything in the Material. Momentum is so very important. A handy document presented to a witness in impeachment is impressive to watch. A fumbling search through disparate case briefs is not.

This leads to a suggestion. Junior counsel should prepare a witness brief of Material as a companion to the outline. This would have its own tabs, each consisting of the relevant pages or other references. Each would be admissible into evidence in its own right. Some or all tabs would already be admitted, with the others to be admitted. This way the witness brief can replace all the other document briefs while the witness is in preparation (if your own witness) or during testimony (any witness). Counsel, the witness and the court can concentrate on the witness brief and ignore the mountain of other documents. This technique is canvassed in greater detail in a later chapter on how junior counsel can help senior litigators in their firms.

A GUIDE TO THE PREPARATION OF THE WITNESS

The outline of the questions that the lawyer will ask at trial can also be the outline of the preparation session. The witness gives answers to the questions. The lawyer then adjusts the outline to accomplish the objectives. By asking these questions again, revised, the lawyer helps the witness to advance the case.

This is not possible when preparing to examine a witness in discovery or in cross-examination at trial. It is possible to "game" the examination with an associate, but it is less likely that this will achieve as much as thoughtful anticipation of what will happen.

The witness brief described above is helpful here. The witness can take it home to prepare for the session with the lawyer. After the session, the witness can use it to prepare for trial.

EXAMPLE FROM THE CASE STUDY

Before we give the proposed answer, try to create an outline that would permit you to examine Lee in chief with respect to the meeting between Kim and Lee. This occurred the day after Kim met Brian in hospital. Compare this to the outline of the same set of questions, asked of Kim. Note that the perspective of the two witnesses is different. Therefore the outline pursues different lines.

Create a headline and several points to be covered within the headline that together will cover the subject.

In the outline that follows, the words "broad to narrow" suggest a wide, open question. If the witness (Lee) misses any of the points that follow, these should be covered with follow-up questions. As such, the outline represents a checklist of points that the witness should cover before leaving the topic.

Heading: Lee meet Kim re Brian

Headline: meeting with Kim on January 12

- What happened at the meeting (broad to narrow)

- Lee's goals for the meeting

- Kim's explanation

- Power of attorney

- Kim's responsibility

- Capacity of Brian

- Hospital situation

- Ken's timetable to complete project

- Next step planned

Now consider the item, "hospital situation". This could be a separate headline to explore during the examination. Remember that the questions are directed to Lee that will flesh out what was discussed with Kim in the meeting of January 12.

- What did Lee ask Kim?

- What did Kim answer?

- What would a third party (expert) say ought to have been discussed?

Heading: hospital situation

Headline: what Lee asked Kim because the meeting was in the hospital

- Layout of the room

- Proximity of other patients

- Health treating professionals nearby

- Situation of the bed in the room

- Hook-up to oxygen or liquids, other inputs

- Brian's health (asked or apparent)

It can be seen that the initial outline of the interview could, by itself, comprise several headlines, each with its own bundle of nested questions.

CHAPTER 4: DISCOVERY AND DEPOSITIONS, PART 1 – BACK STORY

- *In some jurisdictions, just the opposing parties. In some, any significant witness for the opposition.*

- *Combination of direct and cross-examination style of examination.*

- *The examiner does not (likely) know what the witness will say.*

- *Outlines must allow for the unknown.*

GOALS OF THE EXAMINATION

An examination for discovery or deposition (the terms are used interchangeably here) can have several goals.

- To learn what the witness has to say.

- To lock in the witness' testimony for damage control.

- To prove or support some of the elements of your theory.

- To challenge some of the elements of the opposition's theory.

- To support or attack the testimony of other witnesses.

- To attack the witness' credibility, although there may be some restrictions imposed by the local rules.

The subject of discovery examinations is dealt with in much greater length in the handbook in the Young Advocates Series, published by Irwin Law, *Discovery Techniques*. The purpose of this chapter is to discuss outline techniques for discovery.

Counsel cannot know everything the witness will say. There should be flexibility built into the outline to permit exploration. Unlike a tightly scripted cross-examination, counsel may have to change some parts of the outline of the discovery to exploit opportunities provided by the witness. That said, the outline represents the battle plan for the examination. As Mike Tyson said about boxing matches, discovery plans tend to change as the event begins.

Remember to use headlines. These introduce the context. A neutral headline can avoid objections on the basis of relevance.

Flexibility helps in another respect. At the time of the deposition, counsel may not yet have determined the theme, theory and trial strategy. Often, these are still works in progress. The lawyer who conducts the deposition may not be the same one who conducts the trial. It keeps their options open when counsel explore somewhat, not only attack.

START WITH THE BACK STORY

Unless the only plan is to cross-examine to destroy, counsel should start with questions about the witness and how the witness fits into the case. At trial, opposing counsel will try to bolster the theory with facts that make the court accept the witness' testimony. Age, education, family, history in the community and good works - these all may play to the innate bias in all of us, judges included.

None of these facts is part of the elements of the case. In the case study, Kim's age is not relevant to whether there was a breach of duty (or any of the other issues). However, age suggests experience. Experience suggests competence. Competence is very much a part of the breach of duty. Here is an example, age, in which the back story may influence one of the important elements.

Back story questions are easy to ask. They are easy to answer. Perhaps there is a reason not to ask easy questions at the outset of the examination? If so, start elsewhere. Why would you want to start with the high, hard stuff (a baseball reference for attack mode)? If you know that the case turns on one narrow issue, you might want to attack that issue immediately. The witness may react differently after becoming accustomed to the give-and-take by some easy questions.

So, back to the back story. It should not be arduous to imagine what factors may influence a court's decision-making. These can be wrapped into a few headlines that require little in the way of prompts.

The oral headline might be, "First off, let's talk about you." What would you need to prompt you to say that? You might write the word "Biography". If there is a key fact you should not forget, insert a word as a prompt. The typical questions in this section include age, education, relevant training, and work history before the events in issue.

EXAMPLE FROM THE CASE STUDY

Before we give the proposed answer, try to create an outline that would permit you to examine Kim with respect to the back story.

Create a headline and several points to be covered within the headline that together will cover the subject. This may serve as a template for this kind of back story inquiry in other cases.

The purpose is to understand Kim's background. Where does this witness fit in the case? What should counsel know about Kim to be able to formulate a back story that will advance the examiner's case?

Heading/Headline: Kim's background

- Age and residence

- Highest education

- Training in wills and estates

- Training to test for capacity

- Experience for either

Is there anything else to learn about Kim that might be helpful?

As with the earlier exercises, each of these points could form a headline, with nested questions within. Consider the "training to test for capacity".

Headline: test for capacity

- Where and when learned

- From whom

- When implemented or practiced

- Describe the test

CHAPTER 5: DISCOVERY AND DEPOSITIONS, PART 2 – CONTEXT

- *After the back story, the next subject sets context for the events in issue.*

- *There may be points to make, so consider leading questions*

BRIDGE FROM THE BACK STORY TO THE RELEVANT EVENTS

In depositions, there is no technical requirement for a bridge from one section to another. The examiner can ask anything on point. With headlines, relevance is obvious. Once the back story is covered (previous chapter), the next order of business is to identify the situation in which the events occurred, the context.

In the case study, the relevant events began with Brian's admission to City Hospital. This prompted the call to Lee and Associates. If Kim is the witness in the discovery, the examination has to situate Kim in the office in December. How did that happen, the examiner wants to discover?

Discovery is unlike trial examinations, because it can help but never hurt. This means that only the examiner gets to use the transcript at trial, unless the transcript is admitted into evidence for some exceptional reason.

The outline for the discovery should contain a separate section after the back story and before the events in issue. This bridge should accomplish several objectives:

- It allows the examiner to show that the set up to the events was acceptable or defective, somehow, as the spin warrants. The disaster that occurred later was, or was not (as the case may be) a consequence of some inadequacy early on.

- The examiner has not started to cross-examine, and so does not have the active opposition of the witness. It is possible for the examiner to obtain admissions at this stage, which might not occur during destructive cross-examination mode (which might follow later).

- The bridge may expose areas to examine that the examiner had not considered in preparation of the outline.

As with other areas of the outline, the bridge should start with a headline. An example for the deposition of Kim in the case study might be "now let's move on to when you looked for work."

As with the introductory section, each of the items identified in your outline might be the subject of several subordinate points. Each of these might have a headline followed by several questions.

EXAMPLE FROM THE CASE STUDY

Before we give the proposed answer, try to create an outline that would permit you to examine Kim with respect to the start of employment with Lee and Associates.

Create a heading/headline and several points to be covered within the headline that together will cover the subject.

The purpose is to understand how Kim started with Lee. This will be important to deal with Kim's testimony but also with Lee's. Lee had some responsibility to determine Kim's competency, and to provide training and guidance commensurate with Kim's duties.

The focus here will be on the early elements of the case theory. "Kim works for Lee" is an element in the case for all parties. What did Lee do to ensure Kim was a capable wills lawyer?

There may be documentary disclosure prior to the examination. Whether counsel mark the relevant documents as exhibits is a matter of local practice.

Each of these points may form the basis for another headline with several questions. We will look at the job offer in particular.

Heading/Headline: Kim's start with Lee

- Application for position

- Position advertised (exhibit?)

- Due diligence by Kim
- By Lee
- All interviews
- References
- Job offer (exhibit?)
- Contract (exhibit?)
- Promises of training
- Scope of duties

Headline: job offer

- How made
- When
- Response
- Negotiation
- Terms proposed, accepted
- Flexibility

CHAPTER 6: DISCOVERY AND DEPOSITIONS, PART 3 – THE MAIN EVENT(S)

- *After the backstory and the set up, the deposition turns to the events in issue.*

- *Sequence becomes a matter of strategy.*

- *Separate events should be movable based on the responses given.*

OUTLINING THE SEQUENCE OF EVENTS

After the deposition has completed the context, the events begin. How the lawyer puts the events into sequence is very much a matter of strategy. This should be a subject of some thought.

- Does the outline start, chronologically, with the earliest event?

- Does it flow naturally from where the context was introduced?

- Does it flow from the chapter headings of the cause of action?

- Does it follow the pleading of one or other of the parties?

All of these are legitimate sequence choices. This is equally true at trial as it is in depositions. Again, the order of sequence in the questions asked in the deposition is less important than it is at trial.

Remember the three purposes of the deposition, to learn what the party or witness has to say, to support your case and to attack theirs. The result is a transcript that both informs the lawyer and locks the witness into a position upon which the lawyer can rely at trial.

STRATEGY

Once the sequence has been determined, the outline should look at each discrete series of events. Perhaps there was a set of correspondence, followed by a meeting, followed by more correspondence. In that case, the outline might deal with those three subjects - correspondence, meeting, correspondence. Each would have its own headline, followed by a set of questions that identifies the subject, followed by introduction of exhibits (if appropriate).

Consider all of the following questions that flow from the introduction of a document.

- Who wrote it?

- Who else contributed to it?

- When and why was it written?

- When and how was it received?

- What other relevant context is there for the creation of the document?

- To whom did the witness communicate with respect to the document?

- What drafts or other copies are there?

- Where was it sent, when and why?

- Why those recipients and not others?

- What was the reaction of the witness to delivery of the document?

There are other questions that could flow from the introduction of the document. There are questions that flow from the answers given to any of the above questions.

The outline cannot deal with all of the possible follow-up questions. Nor should it. The purpose of the outline, once again, is to prompt the examiner to think. The outline enables the examiner to ask the next question or set of questions. What notes does the examiner need to stay on message? This is very much a matter of personal taste, as some lawyers find a detailed outline to be constructive. Others see it as less necessary, or even as distracting.

TEMPLATES

Depositions often involve repetition from earlier iterations. The event in question may be followed by a similar event at a different time or place or involving different people. The same follow-up questions can be expected, subject to variations based upon specific answers.

In this case, the outline could form a template for use in many situations. The outline for three events (such as meetings, calls, emails) could be identical. Whatever helps the lawyer during the examination.

EXAMPLE FROM THE CASE STUDY

Before we give the proposed answer, try to create an outline that would permit you to examine Carol in discovery with respect to her visits in the hospital with her uncle, Brian.

Create a heading/headline and several points to be covered within the headline that together will cover the subject.

It is unclear whether Carol manipulated Brian or Kim in some way. Clearly, Carol had a vested interest in the failure of Brian's intention to change his will. Consider that it is likely that Carol's visits were similar, one to the other. This set will therefore become a template for each of the visits to follow.

Heading: Carol - hospital

Headline: visit to Brian in City Hospital

- (First) visit - when: December

- Brian's condition

- Mental capacity

- Discussion with treatment providers

- Brian's ability to communicate

- Discussion about will, if any

- Brian's requests of Carol

As with the earlier exercises, each of these could be a headline in its own right, with questions. Let's look at "Brian's ability to communicate".

Headline: Brian's ability to communicate

- Time of day and links of visit

- Use of language

- Clarity of thought

- Known medication

- Variation with time of day or length of visit

- Input by Carol

- Dealing with health treatment providers

- Role of Louise

- Other relatives or visitors

CHAPTER 7: DISCOVERY AND DEPOSITIONS, PART 4 – SPECIFIC QUESTION METHODS

- *Open questions are to learn information.*

- *Closed questions are to confirm admissions and positions.*

- *Leading questions are to attack those positions.*

OPEN QUESTIONS

During the outline, the examiner wants to learn (discover) what the witness has to say about several issues. These issues should be canvassed with open questions and follow-up techniques. Broad-to-narrow starts. Who, what when, where, why and how to complete each sequence.

These techniques are explored in detail in the handbook, **Discovery Techniques** and presently in the **Examinations** handbooks in the Young Advocates Series

This part of the outline should focus on each of the relevant subjects, with appropriate follow-up to ensure the position is explored fully. In fact, this resembles the outline for a direct examination. Because it is a deposition, the examiner has not prepared the witness for the examination. This means that headlines become more important. Questions should be restricted to the headline. The purpose is to keep the witness on track, and without confusion.

The second purpose of this technique is to "feed the transcript". The deposition will be used later, during negotiations, during pretrial conference and during trial itself. That transcript should be orderly, and useful. All of the testimony relevant to a given subject should be found in one place. This makes it easier for the lawyer later to search for it, and then to use it.

CLOSED QUESTIONS

Remember that the difference between a closed question and a leading one is that the former can be answered with a restricted set of answers, but the latter forces a single answer. Deviation from that answer triggers impeachment. Effectively, the examiner puts words into the mouth of the witness.

The outline for the deposition should list all of the points to be made in detail. Because the examiner is pushing a point, the question should come fluidly. The examiner should be in no doubt as to the sequence of questions on the points to be made. The outline should have sufficient detail to accomplish this.

During the discovery examination, the lawyer may want to switch from open questions to closed questions on the fly. It may not be possible to predict when this will occur. This is one of the reasons why lawyer should listen carefully to the answers given by the witness. Even so, lawyers can predict where this might occur. The outline should take this into account, with short, closed questions to establish the points.

LEADING QUESTIONS

There are two situations where counsel lead during depositions. The first is where the matters are entirely noncontroversial. Age, address, occupation and such. It is faster to ask these in a leading form than any other. Time is valuable, and this technique saves time.

The second situation is where counsel want to cross examine. Leading questions are intended to score points for the transcript. They can be very persuasive. Leading questions should be used sparingly, as the lawyer wants to know what will be said at trial as well as to make the points.

Lawyers hate surprises. The leading question may prevent the witness from giving a full answer. At trial, the witness will give that full answer. When the lawyer tries to impeach, the carefully prepared witness may respond, "But you never gave me the chance to say this at the deposition." This is a lawyer's nightmare.

EXAMPLE FROM THE CASE STUDY

One issue between the parties is whether Kim either could or should have had Brian write a short will or codicil to change his gift. Clearly, Kim did not do this. Therefore, the lawyer for Louise may want to make this point at the discovery.

Here is an exercise to give you an appreciation for the impact between asking these questions as open, closed or leading. Prepare an outline using a common headline. Set out the series of questions to get this evidence prompting for open questions. Then, repeat the exercise using closed questions. Finally, repeat the exercise with leading questions.

In each case, the outline will start with the headline: options in the hospital

Open questions

- Why not handwrite new will?

- Why not codicil?

- Discuss with Lee about these options?

The open questions to be asked might look like this:

- Holographic wills are possible in your jurisdiction. Why did you not recommend this to your client?

- You knew about the possibility of codicils. Why did you not recommend this to your client?

- When you returned to your office, what discussion did you have with Lee about these two options?

- What did Lee recommend that you do?

Closed questions

- No holographic will.

- No codicil.

- No discussion with Lee about either.

The closed questions asked on discovery might look like this:

- Did you suggest to Brian that he handwrite a short, new will?

- Did you suggest to Brian that you prepare a short codicil for his signature?

- Did you discuss these options with Lee on your return to the office?

Any of these closed questions could be followed with another question, "why not?"

Leading questions

- No holographic will.

- No codicil.

- No discussion with Lee about either.

The leading questions asked on discovery might look like this:

- You did not advise that Brian prepare a holographic will, correct?

- You did not prepare a short codicil for his signature, correct?

- And you did not discuss either option with Lee, correct?

These questions could be followed up with a further leading question, "You knew each of those to be an option, correct? And your client likely did not, is that correct?"

Note how the outlines for the closed questions and leading questions are identical. As another exercise, prepare questions to establish that Kim could have prepared a will at the office and returned to hospital with a clerk that day. Clearly, this was not done. Why not?

CHAPTER 8: DISCOVERY AND DEPOSITIONS, PART 5 – USING THE PLEADINGS

- *The pleadings matter, both the facts and the law.*

- *They serve as an outline structure option, or as a section within the outline.*

- *They contain admissions.*

- *Ignore the pleadings at your peril!*

WHAT IS IN A PLEADING?

Competent pleaders limit their pleading to the seven elements, the necessary facts upon which to base the claim. There is no need to plead law, as the courts have ruled repeatedly. So, why is it that modern pleadings extend over many pages, with headings and executive summaries?

Pleadings should recite all of the elements of the theory of the party's case. Failure to cover all the bases for an actionable cause of action exposes the party to a non-suit. **Donoghue v. Stevenson** was just such a non-suit, as there was no actionable link between consumer and manufacturer (at least, when the claim began).

Consider what pleadings don't say. Pleadings often seem prolix, but may omit some facts or positions. These omissions can be telling. In the case study, why was Carol not named as a defendant? All the relevant events from Brian's hospital admission through to the call to Lee and

Associates' office in late January involve Carol. Carol clearly benefited from how the story played out. *Cui bono* (who gained)? Carol did.

The case study contains old school pleadings, of the **Odgers on Pleading**[1] variety. Compare these to modern pleadings of ten or more pages to deliver the same substance.

Pleadings now represent an opportunity to persuade. They are often the "first impression" that counsel exploit to pitch their wares. As distasteful this may be to purists, it seems the marketing world has taken over the pleadings process. We can object, or we can take advantage of the opportunity this innovation presents.

HOW CAN A PLEADING SERVE AS THE OUTLINE?

Examine a modern pleading and you will glean much information of use. Anything stated in a pleading can be used as the basis to cross-examine the party, for example. Factual admissions can come back to haunt the party as the case evolves.

It is a not far-fetched idea to create a discovery outline based on the pleading, 100%. Consider the possible approach of defence counsel using this method.

- Start with the claim for relief: how is the amount calculated? If the claim includes equitable relief, exactly what is sought?

- Proceed to the parties. This is the opportunity to explore the back story.

- Then, introduce the events. This sets up the context.

Have you noticed the similarity to the structure set out in the earlier chapters? This is no coincidence. Pleadings typically adopt the format of the seven elements of any case.

- The events that support the cause of action follow the context. Ask about each, with follow-ups as appropriate.

- The next order of business is the legal connection between the events and the cause of action. While discovery is restricted to evidence, there is nothing wrong with testing the legal theory. What other facts or evidence support connection? If there are other facts, not pleaded, the examiner can use them as a springboard to explore or attack as they emerge in the examination for discovery. If the cause of action is restricted to the facts described to that point, the lawyer should have no surprises at trial.

- Damages or consequences of the conduct come next. From the described events, what damages flowed? How were they foreseeable (if that is a relevant concept)? How were they mitigated? How could they have been?

- If the witness is the party, there are several concluding matters to be canvassed. What expert evidence is there? What other witnesses, documents? The list of these concluding questions varies among jurisdictions and local practices.

The approach of plaintiff's counsel to the deposition of the defendant will not be as simple. This is because the defence pleading rarely flows so smoothly as does the claim. Defendants have to deal with the plaintiff's theory and advance their own theory.

IF THE PLEADING DOES NOT SET THE STRUCTURE, WHAT IS ITS ROLE?

At the least, the outline should accommodate the theory expressed in the opposition pleading. Counsel ignore a theory at their own (and their clients' peril). If the plaintiff pleads a link between the consumer to the manufacturer (**Donoghue v. Stevenson**), counsel should ask about that link. What evidence supports the existence of this manufacturer's duty of care to this consumer (if so found)?

Any sentence or paragraph in a pleading can provoke a headline and several questions. Counsel can fit them into the outline seamlessly. Should the testimony contradict the pleading, counsel can use the pleading to impeach (either then or at trial).

USE FOR DEPOSITION OF NON-PARTIES

It may not be obvious where a witness fits into the theory of the case (theirs or yours). If so, that should be the first order of business. All witnesses must contribute something to the elements. Otherwise they should not be named, and would not be called. You initial questions should identify the witness. Then, situate the witness into the context of the case. What characters? What events? Where to start?

Once the deposition establishes where the witness fits, the backstory questions follow the context, not the pleadings. From there, however, the outline could follow the part of the pleadings to which the witness can contribute. It may be prudent to ask the witness to confirm that the other facts pleaded are beyond the witness' knowledge.

Keep in mind that the witness may be asked to confirm or deny what others have said or might say. This will be useful at trial when applying the rule in ***Browne v. Dunn***. The outline should therefore cover what others have to say about the pleadings.

EXAMPLE FROM THE CASE STUDY

Using the Statement of Defence, act for Louise. Create an outline of the discovery of a defendant (Kim or Lee). With each heading, present several sub-headings that flow from it. Think of how to incorporate Lee's interview with Kim within that outline. Does it fit naturally? Review it to find areas that you would include were you to adopt another structure.

- Heading: the parties. In this section, we identify the defendants, their relationship, and their competence as wills practitioners. Sub-headings would include the competency of Kim, and the training and experience undertaken by Kim prior to the consultation of January 2015.

- Heading: history with Brian. In this section, we identify Brian's history with the defendants prior to December 2014. We ask for a copy of his earlier will, together with the notes and records that Lee may have kept with respect to that file. Sub-headings would include recollection of Brian's reasons for omitting Louise, role of Carol in arranging earlier will execution.

- Heading: Brian's request for this consultation. In this section, we explore the initial communication between Carol for Brian and Lee and Associates in December. In doing so, we explore the workings of the law office, and the respective roles of each of the people who played a role with respect to Brian's request. Sub-headings might include the practice of the law firm to deal with requests such as this, experience of dealing with clients in hospital or in other out-of-office settings. Specific sub-heading to deal with Kim or Lee's experience of codicils, holographic wills and other possible stopgap measures that Kim did not adopt.

- Heading: the role of Carol. In this section, we explore all of the communications between Carol and the defendants. We establish what the basis was for each communication, and each action undertaken as a result of Carol's communications. Each has its own sub-heading. We challenge the theory that Carol was in a conflict of interest or that Carol owed the obligation of a lawyer. How could Carol know what could or should be done?

- Heading: the duty of care. In this section, we explore the factual basis that gives rise to a duty of care on the part of a lawyer. When does/did it start?

In this jurisdiction, is there an existing duty of care owed by the lawyer to possible beneficiaries? What is the required factual basis for that duty? If there is no such existing duty, what would be the basis to create one? These would all form sub-headings to be pursued.

- Heading: consequences. In this section, we observed that Lee and Associates handled the probate application. This can establish what the level of damages might be. We also establish that the law firm was quite content to take instructions from Carol, so conflict of interest was known to Lee, but did not raise a red flag.

CHAPTER 9: DIRECT EXAMINATIONS, PART 1 – PREPARATION OF THE CLIENT TO TESTIFY

- *You should have all of the relevant facts.*

- *You have all the time in the world to practice.*

- *You should have a motivated, cooperative witness*

- *There should be no surprises.*

There are three kinds of witness that counsel produce during their case: their client, lay witnesses and expert witnesses. This handbook deals with the first two. The expert witness, as a subject, deserves its own handbook.

INTRODUCING THE CLIENT

In the case of the client as a witness, you have the best of both worlds. You have the time to prepare with the witness and you have a motivated witness. These two conditions are not always the case with the other two categories of witness.

The outline for the examination in chief starts with the preparation of the witness to testify. It then changes to prepare the lawyer going into trial. The two phases involve different considerations.

Consider the purposes of the first outline, the preparation phase.

- Your job is to develop teamwork with the witness, your client.

- Of course, you want to reassure your client that the case has merit.

- You want to show your client that you are competent.

- You want to demonstrate that there is every reason to believe in the success of the outcome of the case.

- The real purpose, from your point of view as a technician, is to develop your witness to perform as well as possible on the witness stand. How can you do this?

Unless your client is a "backwater" witness, one who does not contribute to the case materially, your client should be a major proponent of the theme and theory of your case. This means that your client should understand where you are trying to go, and why. This involves bringing your client inside the tent of case analysis.

It also means that your client should be aware of the case of the opposition. Remember that your opponent has both a theme and a theory to counteract yours. Ignore these at your client's peril.

There is a danger that your client will become an advocate for your position. Advocacy is your job. Your client should stick to the facts, as much as possible. The danger here is that your client will sound over-rehearsed, robotic, repeating the party line. In preparation, you should work with your client to avoid these dangers.

Back to the outline of the meeting with your client to prepare. It should be broken into three sections.

- The first is context. You should explain to the client what you are trying to do and how. If the client does not know how trials operate, now is the time for orientation.

- The second is the outline of the examination that you intend to use at trial. Warn your client that this is a work in process, and that you will make changes based upon how the preparation proceeds.

- The third is the inoculation phase. You should prepare your client to be cross-examined, or to face questions from the trial judge.

CONTEXT OF THE EXAMINATION

You will probably have an opportunity to meet with your client more than once. It is common practice to establish the context in the first preparation session, but not again after that. It is helpful for some clients to break the preparation sessions into two or more segments, separated by some period of time. It is a judgment call on the part of the trial lawyer as to how much preparation each client requires. Over-preparation is a danger by itself.

The outline of your preparation may form a template. How do you prepare all of your clients to testify? Or all of your clients for this kind of case? Lawyers try to train their clients right from the initial interview. Each one requires something from each of the following elements:

- What is the theme of your case? Here you will discuss how the case appears, and how you are trying to make your point. How will you deliver the message effectively?

- What is the theory of your case? Without spending too much time on the technical aspects of the legal issues, establish what points are necessary for your case to succeed.

- What is the position of your opponent? Both their theme and theory are important here. How do they differ from yours? It is rarely a case of black and white. They may agree with some of your elements. They may just spin them differently.

- What are you trying to accomplish with the practice sessions? Clients want to know what they are doing and why. They also want to know what role they are expected to play during the trial. Many do not know that their contact with witnesses is restricted by local rules of practice.

- How can things go wrong? The idea is to warn the client that cases rarely proceed as planned. This uncertainty is a great settlement driver.

- What will go on in the courtroom? Many clients think that trials are reflected by what they see on television. Disabuse them of this notion.

- How will the case proceed? Lay out for the client what witnesses you intend to call, what witnesses the opposition may call. Show the client the expected flow of direct, cross and redirect, objections, exhibits and the like.

- How should the client behave? It is commonplace for lawyers to give their clients short videos with "Testimony do's and don'ts", tips of general application. Such tips might include how to dress, how to address the court, where to sit or stand, and the basics of testimony. Some clients will watch them and learn, while others will not. Some clients benefit from watching the video repeatedly. A benefit of the video is that the lawyer does not have to cover this subject in meetings with the client. Another benefit us that the video should assure the client of the lawyer's competence and presence.

INOCULATION

There is a challenge that faces the client's lawyer before the preparation session with the client. How can the lawyer predict the cross-examination that will follow the client's testimony? Ideally, the lawyer will prepare a full cross-examination for the client as if conducted by the opposition. Ideally, the outline of this covers the highlights of what will occur at trial. The client should not be surprised by a line of questions asked in cross.

The cross-examination should cover the theme and theory of the opposing party. Indeed, this is one of the main reasons why lawyers undertake full case analysis before the trial.

The client is the main sales person for the case. That also means that the client can be the weakest link. The outline of the preparation should account specifically for exactly this weakness.

There is a danger that the client will be frightened by a successful cross-examination during the preparation session. To some extent, a healthy respect for the case of the opposition is a good thing. It encourages settlement. It avoids overconfidence. This again is a fine line for the trial lawyer's judgment. Usually, it strengthens the performance of the client as a witness.

EXAMPLE FROM THE CASE STUDY

There are three clients, Lee, Kim and Louise. Louise is pretty well a backwater. What did she do or observe, that matters? True, she forms much of the back story. And she can testify to her visits with Brian in City Hospital. Altogether, that may be 20 minutes or so.

Lee, Kim and the non-party, Carol, are going to be the principal witnesses. Let's assume that Kim is our client. Prepare the outline of the preparation for Kim before trial, including inoculation.

From the outline below, could you prepare Kim for a complete direct examination? What more would you require? How would any of the headings or points change if Lee were the witness?

Backstory

- Education
- Training pre-Lee
- Job search

Start with Lee

- Role
- Office setup
- Training
- Experience before Brian

Brian's earlier will

- Hospital
- Urgency?
- Roles within office

December call from Carol

- Office practice
- Explain roles and actions
- Next step?

January call

- Date
- Spoke to Carol

- Plans due to hospital

- Discuss with Lee before

Meet Carol

- Where, when

- Discuss, POA

- To Brian

Meet Brian

- Carol role

- Setting in hospital

- Brian's apparent health

- Other patients

Discussion with Brian

- Perform tests for capacity

- Why not

- Gist of intentions

- POA

- Urgency

Retainer

- Directions for will signing

- Lawyer-client yet

- When

- Legal advice

- What next step

- Timing

Meet Lee

- When, how long

- Why

- Discussion

- Advice

Preparation of will

- When planned

- Explain

Learn of death

- Warning

- Aware of mortality

Inoculation

- Why no holographic will

- Why no codicil

- Why not prepare will same day

- Why not involve Lee more

- Why not ask about health issues of Brian

CHAPTER 10: DIRECT EXAMINATIONS, PART 2 – THE CLIENT IN CHIEF

- *Outline follows the seven elements of the theory.*

- *Client is often the best way to present the story to the court.*

- *Practice is rewarded by performance.*

The direct examination of the client should be the highlight of the case. Unfortunately, this is not always true. The reason is that the client is often the focus for the most rigorous cross-examination.

THE CLIENT AS SELLER, MC

Clients are often knowledgeable about all aspects of the theory of the case. They are the ones who suffered the damage, or are alleged to have caused it. They are the ones who know about the duty, whether in tort or in contract. They are the ones who were involved in the alleged breach. The thrust of the client's direct examination should be to "sell" the case. An exception the nominal "client", such as a tort case where the defendant is insured.

The client can also serve as a form of introduction to the other witnesses, on both sides. Clients often know who the other witnesses are and how they fit into the case. Lawyers should prepare their cases with the possibility that their clients serve as the "Master of Ceremonies" of the case.

Fortunately, lawyers have all the time in the world to prepare their clients for this role. At the time of the trial itself, however, things speed up. Real-time comes into play. Will the client act as predicted?

The outline of the client's examination must therefore reflect the client's ability as a witness. How good is the client as a storyteller? How much prompting will the client need to stay on message? These are relevant to the outline, because the examiner must lead the witness through the evidence.

Inoculation is another focus of the direct examination. Just as the direct examination should be the high point, so could the cross-examination be the low point for the client's case. The client has likely been examined for discovery. This means that there will be few surprises to the cross-examiner, who plays the role of predator. The cross-examiner will be prepared for virtually anything the client - the prey - might say in the direct examination.

While the cross-examiner may have some surprises in store for the witness, case analysis should arm the direct examiner to prepare the witness to withstand the assault. In the practice sessions, the examiner should have introduced the client to the likely attacks, whether on issues of fact or of credibility. These must be reflected in the outline in the inoculation. This could appear either in a separate section or be intermingled in the relevant sections of the direct outline.

It is not necessary that the outline reflect exactly what the preparation outline did. The cues, however, should not confuse the client. They should all be similar to the ones introduced during preparation. If there are major changes between the preparation and trial outlines, the lawyer should introduce these to the client before testimony begins.

Language is important. The answers should reflect the personality of the client. Questions should encourage the client to testify in a credible manner. Counsel should be alert to this objective. Short questions are best, to let the client keep centre stage. Short sequences of questions, each sequence with a headline. This technique will keep the client on message. The outline sculpted for this witness is the perfect tool. Five-and-out technique works just as well in directs as in crosses.

CONNECT THE TESTIMONY OF THE CLIENT TO THE OPENING ADDRESS

The lawyer has likely introduced the court to the theory during the opening. It is helpful to have the first witness, usually the client, testify in line with the lawyer's summary. Clients do not always testify first, but it is quite common. The reason for this is that clients can talk about the whole case. If the client is a backwater witness, the lawyer should lead with another spokesperson.

The opening address likely discussed each of the elements of the theory of the case. The client can then testify about each of the elements identified in the lawyer 's address. This reinforces what the lawyer has just said. The outline of the client's direct could very well follow the exact theory that has just been explained by the lawyer.

EXAMPLE FROM THE CASE STUDY

We will use Lee this time, who is hardly a backwater witness. Lee is one of the parties, and is aware of the elements of the case. And Lee is sophisticated, familiar with legal issues. Lee was not present for some of the important events. This means that Lee can introduce them but may not be able to testify about the detail.

An outline of the direct examination of Lee might be the following. Take a few minutes and try to use this outline as your direct examination of this client-witness. Afterward, ask yourself whether It was sufficient for the task. Was anything missing? Remember that each bullet point is a headline to introduce five or so questions to make the point.

Backstory: Biography of Lee and firm

Context:

- Roles of staff and Lee within the firm

- Introduce Kim

- History with Brian, first will

Relevant events:

- Initial contact with Carol

- Meeting at hospital

- Meeting with Kim

- Learned of death

- Completion of probate

Inoculation:

- Experience of Kim

- Advisory role at meeting following hospital visit

- Delay in preparing the will

- Holographic will or codicil

CHAPTER 11: DIRECT EXAMINATIONS, PART 3 – THE OTHER WITNESSES

- *There is less opportunity to prepare the witness.*

- *The witness does not contribute to all of the elements of the theory.*

- *The outline should reflect the backstory, if applicable, and the relevant elements.*

- *Inoculation is riskier because cross-examination is less predictable.*

THE ROLE OF LAY WITNESSES

The lay witness is often not as committed to the case as is the client. Scheduling - both preparation sessions and the testimony at trial - can be an issue. This witness has a life apart from the litigation. The lay witness may not be able to contribute to as many of the elements of the theory of the case. The lawyer often learns during the preparation phase of the constraints presented by the witness. There are limits, to both the level of cooperation and what the witness can contribute.

There are several reasons for lawyers to approach lay witnesses with care:

- As noted, there is typically less opportunity for the lawyer to prepare with the lay witness.

- It is common for lay witnesses to have an agenda of their own. They may want to divert blame. Or to attack the other party for some reason. Or to accomplish some unknown objective (unknown to the lawyer, at least).

- As this is a witness called by the lawyer, the testimony can be harmful.

- Short of treating the witness as hostile, the lawyer has no remedy should the witness change the story at trial.

In short, there are risks.

Let's assume that the witness is not trying to cause harm to your case. Even so, lay witnesses may not follow the script. They have less at stake. There is less (or no) time for the lawyer to prepare with them. Therefore, they require better cues in the form of headlines. The lawyer should deviate from the cues discussed in advance only rarely. To avoid an objection that the lawyer is leading the witness, the outline should provide the headlines that will keep up the steady momentum of the testimony. It is more important for headlines to be neutral in the case of lay witnesses.

Inevitably, however, the lawyer will have to take some chances. It almost never occurs that the witness stays exactly on message. Therefore, the lawyer is often in a position of having to ask a question to which the answer has not been rehearsed.

SEQUENCE OF WITNESSES

Lawyers have to determine which witness will testify and in what order. Often, this is a function of availability as much as choreography. This issue of trial strategy is beyond the scope of this handbook. However, it is important for lawyers to appreciate what evidence has already been introduced. When the witness testifies, the court may already have heard what other witnesses have had to say on subjects to be covered by this witness. If the client has testified, then it is likely that some of the elements of the case have already been introduced.

Therefore, lawyer should be aware that the witness will likely be cross-examined if that witness deviates from what has already been said in court. Because the witness has not heard what has gone on in court, as is usually the case, the lawyer knows something that the witness does not. Local rules may prevent the lawyer from warning the witness about previous, conflicting testimony. This makes it all the more important for the lawyer to perform proper case analysis before the trial begins. To the extent possible, this case analysis should find its way into the preparation of the witness, the outline and the headlines used.

THEORY OF THE CASE

The witness will contribute something that is relevant to the theory of the case, unless the witness testifies only about the back story. Lawyers often have to build their case with testimony from such witnesses.

In practice sessions, the lawyer should introduce the witness to the elements of the theory of the case to which the witness can contribute. Why is the testimony relevant? How does it help the case? This gives the witness the context within which to understand the questions.

The outline of the examination should reflect the cues necessary to keep the witness on script. The script consists of the relevant elements that the lawyer requires to make the case.

It sometimes happens that lawyers must rely upon opposition witnesses to prove some of the elements of their own theory. For example, only this opposition witness can identify a document or testify it was sent or received. Usually, counsel cannot practice with the opposition's witnesses. "There is no property in a witness." True, but there is no requirement for the witness to talk to opposing counsel, either.

INOCULATION

In practice sessions, the lawyer should prepare each witness to be cross-examined. The witness should understand the context of theoreticians. Where does it fit into the theory? Then, the witness should be able to cope better with cross-examination. This means that the witness can appreciate where the cross-examiner is going.

This leads to a bit of a dilemma. Lawyers do not want their own witnesses to anticipate cross-examination, except in the inoculation phase of the direct examination. This requires too much thought and, sometimes, causes the witnesses to be seen as advocates. A witness who gives long answers to questions that seek short ones may not be credible. This is also true for a witness who appears to explain everything. On the other hand, the witness who gives an admission without realizing it as such, may just sink the case. Ouch.

The outline of the direct examination should therefore include enough inoculation to let the witness explain the weaknesses, as controlled by the lawyer. When the cross-examination occurs, the witness has already testified in the best light possible. Usually, that is the best that the direct examiner can accomplish.

EXAMPLE FROM THE CASE STUDY

Carol is the only witness for whom we have a statement, but who is not a party. Clearly, she may have her own agenda. Clearly, she knows a lot more about the elements of the case than does her sister, Louise.

It is not a foregone conclusion that Carol will testify at the trial. Similarly, it is not clear who will call Carol to testify, the plaintiff or the defense. And Carol may not be happy to help counsel prepare. Remember that Carol has already gotten her inheritance. Things can only go downhill from there.

Let's assume that Carol is to be called by the lawyer for Louise. The outline of her examination might be as follows below. Take a few minutes and try to use this outline to present her direct examination. Assume any answers that you wish. Is this outline sufficient? What is missing?

Remember that each bullet point is a sub-heading. Use it to create a headline to introduce five or so questions to make the point.

Backstory: biography

Context:

- Carol's history with Brian

- Brian's health issues

- Role with his previous will

- Louise' involvement with Brian

Relevant events:

- Brian's admission to hospital

- Carol's role while Brian was in hospital

- Initial call to Lee and Associates

- January call to Lee, Kim

- Meeting in hospital

- Brian's capacity at time of meeting

- Brian's decline at the end of January

- Probate and value of estate

Inoculation:

- Knowledge of mortality issues

- Failure to communicate urgency to Lee or Kim

- Delays

- Absence of Louise

- The overflow room was no place for a legal interview

CHAPTER 12: CROSS-EXAMINATIONS, PART 1 – THE OPPOSING PARTY

- *Start to prepare from the first meeting with the client.*

- *Build on existing or create new theme.*

- *Exploit credibility opportunities.*

- *Should be the low point of opposition's case.*

Unlike the other opposition witnesses, lawyers should know exactly what to expect from the opposing party. Think of all the inputs. Your own client may well know much about the opposing party. You deposed the party. You have a brief of documents produced by the opposing lawyer. You may have learned much about that party from witnesses friendly to your cause.

Even in an insurance case, your client-claimant may have experience dealing with the tort insurer (a stand-in) for the other party. In commercial cases, where the opposing party is a company, association or bureaucracy, there are several sources of information that concern the central figure who will testify as the face of the party.

Discovery and documentary disclosure are designed to avoid surprises at trial. The discovery transcript should contain much of the raw material on which to base the cross-examination. Other witnesses, especially where depositions are permitted of non-parties - may have surfaced to supply information that contributes to the cross-examination. Surveillance may help, as well. How does counsel prepare a cross-examination outline from all of these sources?

WHEN TO BEGIN TO PREPARE?

As soon as a file is opened in a litigation matter, there should be a sub-folder for trial preparation. Eventually, you will have one for all witnesses, both actual and possible. If a thought occurs to you during any stage of the litigation, you should record it in 'trial prep'. Finish your thought. If it concerns a witness, the folder for that witness should store that thought.

Immediately record the questions that allow you to nail the point. Write down the sequence or series of points or punchlines that might allow to to establish the conclusion. Good thoughts can be fleeting. Like a dream that is so vivid, only to be forgotten in the light of day. Capture these thoughts while they are still fresh in your mind. Finish the thought right away. This habit will reward you as the trial date approaches.

This is also true for all of the events that occur as the litigation proceeds. Comments made by opposing or friendly counsel, witness statements, a remark from a mediator or pretrial judge, all of these may inspire an idea for cross-examination. All of these belong in your trial prep and witness folders to exploit when you prepare to cross-examine the opposing party.

As soon as Kim or Lee walks into your office to retain your services, you should be working on how to cross-examine Louise, Carol and, possibly, a second-guessing expert. Your own client is often a good source of inspiration for the attack on the opposing party.

THE EMERGING OUTLINE

As trial approaches, you should subdivide the folders, assigning one file to each witness - on both sides. Assign a sub-folder for each issue, or even each element. These will form the witness part of your trial brief.

As a cross-reference, your thoughts about each element will refer to the witnesses and exhibits you require to make the point (or to attack the opposition's point). Your thoughts about each witness will refer to the elements, the exhibits and the other witnesses. This is the making of your outline.

The outline is a work In progress. Just as was the case with the client and direct witnesses. This time, however, the inputs do not include the preparation with the witness. The transcript of the deposition replaces this. In fact, the transcript is an excellent place to start the outline. How does this work? Try this as a workflow sequence:

- Make a summary of the transcript, with notes to identify what the witness said and where.

- Cross-reference the exhibits, both those mentioned in the transcript and others.

- Cross-reference to what other witnesses have to say.

- Block and paste the summary with the references to the seven elements of the theory, from your case analysis.

- Put the sequence of the elements into an order that makes sense for your cross.

- Refer to your trial prep folder. Insert the points that occurred to you before that relate to this witness. It is likely that each of these was covered in the transcript.

This is not a finished product, any means. It should, however, serve as an excellent first draft. Every point in this new file is one to which the witness has committed. If the witness' testimony at trial differs from your new outline, you have an opportunity to impeach.

POSSIBLE PUNCHLINES AND 5-AND-OUT TECHNIQUE

The YAS handbooks, *Discovery Techniques* and *Examinations* introduce and explain the technique called the "5-and-out". This mechanical formula-based technique can serve as a default technique to score points against a witness, including the opposite party.

In summary, here is the formula:

- Think of a point you want to make, a conclusion you hope that the court will make.

- Introduce the subject with a neutral headline.

- Try to make the point with five (or so) leading questions, to which each answer is "yes".

- Each of the questions should solicit known replies, deviation from which is impeachable. Have your impeachment sources at the ready!

- Do not express the punchline out loud. This should be inferred from the sequence of affirmative answers. The punchline, if asked, might well be the dreaded "question too many".

The handbooks both contain several examples and exercises to demonstrate the technique. The technique's effectiveness can be devastating, the apparent momentum overwhelming.

As you add points to your folders, it is very helpful to create the 5-and-out sequence for each that will nail the point. This may illustrate that the point is difficult to establish. It may identify where further evidence is needed. So, consider another bullet point for the proposed workflow sequence set out above:

- For each point that you want to make, create a five-and-out, complete with heading and headline.

Because the sequence within a 5-and-out sequence is important, it is best to have this spelled out in the outline. Because the answers to the questions are all known, the outline should list all the impeachment sources. They should be at counsel's fingertips to build on the momentum.

SEQUENCE OF POINTS

As trial approaches, counsel should arrange the points to be made on cross into a cohesive outline. The sequence may change from preparation to implementation. We can now observe a major benefit of an outline that contains chapter headings, sub-headings and then 5-and-out points. Counsel can cut and paste a set of points to move it elsewhere, or abandon it altogether.

The sequence must make some sense. The court has to follow the logic of the points. It need not be chronological, only logical. It should not matter if the witness can follow the logic. A good cross-examination will succeed regardless of the witness's ability to predict the next question. Indeed, a witness may well make an admission in the belief that a killer question will follow. Another consideration is that judges tend to distrust witnesses who anticipate questions.

Whatever the sequence, counsel should leave room in the outline to deal with testimony that arises in direct examination. Some counsel prefer to start their cross-examination with the subject the witness finished with in chief. Some counsel prefer to seek a brief recess or to ask aimless questions until the next recess. This provides the chance to review the outline to make the adjustments necessary in light of what transpired during direct examination.

Trial counsel cannot anticipate the reaction of the judge to the testimony in chief. Questions and body language from the Bench may suggest an adjustment to the sequence in the outline. This also applies to the manner in which the witness answers hard questions and questions asked as inoculation. There may be a weakness to exploit. Or, that rest-while killer 5-and-out sequence may have just have become too risky or irrelevant.

THEME

If counsel did a good job on the examination for discovery, the opposition theory has been laid out clearly, and (one hopes) challenged. It is now time to dissect it. There should be a central theme to the attack. This should be reduced to a simple phrase. In the case study, for example, a cross of Louise might focus on:

- Her sense of entitlement ("gold-digger").

- The disproportionate claim of $200,000 for a few surreptitious visits to see Brian in hospital ("money for nothing").

A word of warning. You should have a theme for your own case. Do not use an attack on the opposition that is inconsistent with your own theme. For example, if you want Kim to appear serious and professional, do not use the cross of Louise or Carol to encourage a portrayal of Kim as an innocent novice.

CREDIBILITY

Because of the discovery transcript, counsel will have the greatest opportunity for impeachment. The testimony from all the witnesses for both sides represents ammunition to attack the opposing party. The transcript fixes the position of that party. Any deviation will attract impeachment. This requires that counsel be ready. This means preparation and outlining.

If the transcript reveals something the party has said that helps your case, note it right in your outline. If the party says something else, the outline should prompt an impeachment. You will waste the opportunity (and any momentum) if you scramble to find an elusive reference in a thick transcript or brief of exhibits.

This is not to say that your outline should lay out each step of the impeachment. It is unlikely that the opposing counsel will telegraph the change in testimony. You should learn how to impeach, as explained in the handbook in this series, ***Introduction to Trial Advocacy***. Then, rely on your skill when the opportunity arises at trial.

The rules of practice in some jurisdictions encourage this. If a witness misspeaks in a deposition, counsel may choose to alert the examiner to the error. This, however, becomes a red flag for impeachment.

USE OF TRANSCRIPT TO SET UP IMPEACHMENT

A useful technique is to plug part of the discovery transcript into the outline of your cross. Read each question to the witness at trial as if it were a new question. If there is a deviation, ask the question again. "Are you sure?" The witness has fallen into the impeachment trap.

This technique applies best where ANY of three conditions are met:

- The testimony on discovery was helpful to your case.

- You strongly suspect the witness will not say the same thing now, in a material respect.

- You have another, credible witness who will contradict. ***Browne v. Dunn*** comes into effect here, also canvassed in the ***Introduction to Trial Advocacy*** handbook.

EXAMPLE FROM THE CASE STUDY

We will prepare to cross-examine Lee at trial, on behalf of our client, Louise. There are several points that beg for probing. Let's pretend that you examined Lee for discovery. The following exchange occurred midway through the three-hour session.

Q215. I understand you met with Kim on January 12. Tell me what was discussed.

A. This was Kim's first client intake out of the office. I wanted to know what happened.

Q216. What did Kim tell you?

A. Kim met with the woman who called us, Carol. They met in the lobby. Carol said that she most wanted Kim to arrange for a POA.

Q217. Anything else?

A. Then they went together to the next floor, to Brian's room.

Q218. Anything about the room?

A. I did not ask, and Kim did not say.

Q219. What happened in the room, with Brian?

A. Kim described the POA exchange. Kim suggested it, and Brian refused.

Q220. What else did Kim tell you about the meeting?

A. Brian told Kim the one change he required in his will. Nothing else.

Q221. What did you ask or tell Kim?

A. Kim was concerned that Brian did not understand the importance of the POA to Carol. I told Kim that was Brian's decision, not Carol's. You can lead a horse to water, as they say.

Q 222. What other advice or instruction did you give Kim?

A. None. It was Kim's file.

Q223. Let's be clear, then. So far as you were concerned, was Kim the responsible lawyer on the case?

A. Yes.

In your cross-examination outline, identify a couple of punchlines that arise from this exchange. Then consider how they fit into a theme you could use in a larger strategy. Work the punchlines into 5-and-out sequences, in outline format. Remember the pleading in the Statement of Defence that Brian had not yet retained the firm. The exercise might look like this.

Theme: Lee was asleep at the switch

First punchline: Brian hired Lee, not Kim.

Second punchline: Lee delegated a tough task to an unprepared rookie.

Headline: retainer

- Kim went

- On behalf of Lee & co.

- To change his will

- which Lee had done

- Came back with Brian's instructions

Headline: not discussed in meeting of January 12 - any of:

- Client's health

- Capacity test

- Privacy

- Time to complete will

- Return to hospital that day with codicil

CHAPTER 13: CROSS-EXAMINATIONS, PART 2 – LAY WITNESSES

- *Here is where the surprises are.*

- *Case analysis governs all decisions.*

- *Outlines are a work in progress - not the finished product.*

Despite the rules of disclosure, civil trial counsel usually reveal the minimum. This is a reciprocal default, so neither party can complain. This may not be what the judges and rules-makers want to hear, but it is reality. Outlines for cross-examinations of non-party witnesses become estimates, at best.

PREPARE FOR THE SURPRISE

This heading appears oxymoronic. How do you prepare for, well, what you cannot anticipate? The easy answer, is that you can't, so give yourself the day off. That is awful advice, of course. You see a name on a list provided by opposing counsel, maybe with a brief willsay. Now, you have to guess. An educated guess, mind you. What will the witness say? How will it help their case, hurt your case?

Experienced trial lawyers can recite several anecdotes of their successes (and occasional failures) with surprises that arose during the cross of a lay witness. Usually, although they may not confess this, the surprise was caused by inadequate preparation. No, counsel cannot always predict what such witnesses will say.

If you created the witness file folders suggested earlier, you already have much of the material assembled. Better, you may have some thoughts on cross questions or points. This will be a huge aid in the high-stress days of trial preparation.

Even so, there are usually several sources to assist counsel prepare to cross-examine the lay witness. Your own client and witnesses may know the witness. The context may suggest what the witness will say. Various documents may mention or relate to the witness. In discovery, the witness' name may have surfaced. This reinforces the need to follow up in discovery. Such follow-up should deal with the following subjects. What is the role of the witness? What will the witness say? What documents pertain to the witness? Where was the witness during the events?

In jurisdictions where counsel can depose the opposition's witnesses, the surprise disappears. Then, counsel can prepare in the same way as for the opposing party.

CASE ANALYSIS - THE SAVING GRACE

For the purpose of this chapter, review Chapter 1 of this handbook. Case analysis technique requires the analyst to reduce the case to its bare minimum number of elements (target number around seven). Then the analyst reworks these to support the client's position. Finally, the analyst reworks them to support the opposition.

The opposition calls the lay witness to testify for a reason. That reason is found in the case analysis - usually in the seven elements spun for the opposition. As an example from the case study, perhaps a nurse shows up on Louise' witness list. Probably, this witness will testify about Brian's capacity. The element for the nurse' testimony might be, "Brian had his wits about him." Or maybe the focus will be on the meeting between Kim and Brian in January 11. The element might be, "Kim could easily have had Brian sign a codicil or write out a holographic will." True, this is not one of the elements listed in Chapter 1. Should it be?

To prepare, you could consult the hospital records. What did the witness record in nurse's notes for the day? Assume that the nurse recorded the following: "Brian had a visitor, in business attire with brief case. Met at his bedside for 20 minutes."

With this in hand, you can predict that the witness could testify to the elements of Brian's capacity and the meeting. You could therefore prepare an outline to cross-examine on both of those points.

OUTLINES AS A STARTING POINT

Counsel really cannot commit to a course of action in advance. Perhaps the witness' testimony is not harmful to your case. You might not want to risk any cross at all. Or the witness confirms one element, but not another. Your outline should deal with as many outcomes as you can anticipate.

As with the opposing client, your outline should cross-reference all exhibits and witness testimony or statements that might help. Five-and-out sequences will make your cross effective. They will make you appear to be prepared and professional.

To be safe, you should consult your case analysis. What *could* the nurse testify about that pertains to each of the elements for either side? In the case study example, you could then determine whether the nurse might help you establish part of your case or harm part of Louise' case.

Remember Lee's position: Brian directed that Kim wait for his discharge to complete the will. Surely the nurse can help with Brian's capacity to give this direction?

A NOTE FOR THE TRIAL ITSELF

Remind yourself to take your time. Don't rush into a cross-examination without some thought. Counsel often beat themselves up later for missing out on an opportunity.

Judges will usually grant cross-examiners a brief recess before the cross begins. Two exceptions are brief witnesses and trials that are running late. You can ask for the recess on the promise that it will save time, which is often the case. If you make the promise, deliver the goods to stay on the judge's good side.

Consider the rules of court. If counsel may not speak to their own witness after the cross-examination begins, make sure the judge rules that the cross has begun before the recess. This eliminates the risk that opposing counsel will use the recess to warn the witness of what you might try to do.

EXAMPLE FROM THE CASE STUDY

Two techniques are in play this time. First, determine what elements the nurse might address. Then, create an outline of the two 5-and-out sequences identified above in the 'saving grace' section. Lee and Associates is your client for this exercise.

The following proposal is one approach to the problem. There may well be others. The purpose of the example is to demonstrate what is possible, not what is the best solution. Examinations resemble chess problems in this respect. There may be several methods that work.

First, the case for the defence.

- Brian makes a will leaving his estate to his niece, Carol. Nurse irrelevant.

- Brian gets very sick, confined to hospital. Nurse relevant. Medications and impact of medical condition come into play.

- Brian contacts his lawyer to redo his will. Nurse irrelevant.

- Lee and Associates send Kim to meet Brian. Nurse irrelevant, likely.can nurse testify about Brian's dependence on Carol?

- Due to site conditions in the hospital, Kim cannot perform proper capacity assessment or conduct a proper will intake interview. Leads to conclusion that there is therefore no retainer and no will instruction. Nurse relevant.

- Kim receives instructions to wait until Brian is discharged from hospital. His capacity to give this direction presumed by law. Nurse relevant.

- Brian dies three weeks later, without being discharged or changing his instructions. Nurse relevant to health after January 11 to date of death. Point conceded on death, but not otherwise.

- Carol receives what is rightfully hers, compliant with the written directions of Brian and his only valid will. Nurse irrelevant.

Then, the case for Louise.

- Brian has two nieces, his favorite, Carol, and the estranged Louise. Nurse relevant to visits by Louise.

- Brian makes a will leaving his estate to Carol. Nurse irrelevant.

- Brian gets very sick, confined to hospital, facing his mortality. Nurse relevant.

- Brian has his wits about him. The law presumes this to be true. Nurse relevant.

- Brian reconciles with Louise and wants to make things right by redoing his will. Nurse may be relevant.

- Lee assigns the inexperienced Kim to take instructions to change the will to allocate his estate equally between his beloved nieces. Nurse irrelevant.

- Kim could and should have dealt with this immediately, by doing a new will that day or with a holographic will or codicil prepared in hospital. Nurse relevant to capacity and possibly to circumstances of meeting.

- Brian dies three weeks later, with Lee and Associates doing nothing at all to prepare the will. Nurse relevant to health after January 11 to date of death. Point conceded on death, but not otherwise.

- Louise misses out on what is rightfully hers. Nurse may be relevant to visits by Louise.

Punchline: Kim could not assess Brian's capacity on January 11

Headline: what Kim could observe that day

- Brian was in the overflow room

- Not alone

- No privacy

- Short visit

- Impact of meds not readily visible to strangers

- Lay (non-medical) people could not assess condition

- Nurse not familiar with legal capacity test for wills (may be separate sequence)

Punchline: if Brian capable to do will, he was capable to direct delay

Headline: Brian's capacity that day

- Brian able to converse

- Brian was aware of his health issues

- Was Carol (closed question format. Although harmless, it may assist an attack on Carol as keeping secrets from Kim for her own agenda.)

- No idea if Kim was aware of Brian's health

- Brian could give sensible directions

- To Kim

CHAPTER 14: HOW TO PREPARE AN OUTLINE FOR A SENIOR LITIGATOR

- *Junior associates can add real value.*

- *Case analysis, again.*

- *Forces the associate to think like a tactician.*

- *Allows the associate into the team tent.*

WHY DO SENIOR LITIGATORS DELEGATE TO JUNIORS?

Really, this is a fair question. It often takes more time for senior lawyers to delegate and do quality assurance than to do the work delegated. There are two good reasons to delegate. First, to train the junior to improve in the hope that the opportunity cost of delegation reduces overtime. The second is because the junior can add value.

Value appears in the form of a quality piece of work. Also, in the form of the second opinion that follows when a bright professional considers the case afresh. So what is the senior looking for?

While the senior likely wants the junior to think like the senior, most seniors genuinely want another view. So long as that view is thoughtful.

ENTER CASE ANALYSIS

We are beating a dead horse, you say. Not so, is the reply. The senior may well not have had the time to think through the case with the logical discipline required by case analysis.

- What are the seven elements of our case?

- How can we prove them?

- How can the opposition attack them?

- How about their case?

The senior has several files and demands on time. The case, if a huge one, has many sub-issues, each of which has witnesses, documents. Each case and issue beg for analysis.

Consider the *Scott Schedule* required in modern construction litigation files, starting in the UK, but prevalent across Canada and Australia. This is a complex grid of issues that informs the court what issues have what witnesses, exhibits and places of disagreement. Perfect ground for a well-trained junior associate to add value. In fact, most modern commercial litigation requires the effort implicit in a *Scott Schedule*.

Senior lawyers instinctively consider the opposition's case. A junior who goes through the exercise of laying it out, complete with spin, confirms that instinct. Or improves on it with the rigour of the technique. How impressive is that?

WHERE THE JUNIOR ASSOCIATE ADDS REAL VALUE

The layout of the examination, whether deposition, direct or cross, should reflect the objectives of the senior. But here is where the junior has the time and discipline to add real value. The junior can:

- Assemble all the exhibits and assign them to their respective elements.

- Consider all the possible witnesses and assign their likely testimony to their respective elements.

- Look for weaknesses in the expected testimony of the witness to be outlined, either to prepare a cross or to inoculate.

- Identify the punchlines to be accomplished.

- Arrange them in a logical sequence.

- Compile the 5-and-out sequences for each punchline.

- Assign the exhibits and other witnesses to their relevant sequences.

- Identify impeachment opportunities.

- Research possible explanations for impeachments.

- Consider possible deviations from expected testimony, and plan tactics to deal with these.

- Create the issue and witness folders that contain thoughts about each issue or witness.

THE WITNESS BRIEF

In an earlier chapter on general outline structure, it was suggested that counsel should prepare a witness brief of Material as a companion to the outline. Here are the attributes of this brief:

- It has its own tabs, for ease of reference.

- Each tab consists of the relevant pages or other referenced documents.

- Each should be admissible into evidence in its own right.

- Some tabs would already be admitted, either by this witness or by earlier ones.

- The others would be introduced into evidence through this witness or later ones, to be admitted.

- Each tab refers to the exhibit number or name or other reference point.

- Each tab has its reference to the outline of this witness.

- If permitted by local rules, each has highlighter or Post-it Notes to focus the attention of the witness, counsel and court.

The glory of this technique is that this smaller brief can replace all the other document briefs while the witness is on the stand. Counsel, the witness and the court can concentrate on the witness brief and ignore the mountain of other documents. In litigation database software, the witness brief and its annotations are searchable.

Junior counsel can add real value to a senior litigator by preparing a witness brief alongside the outline. It is a time-consuming task that requires acorn inaction of diligence, thoroughness and imagination. What a perfect recipe for an eager junior associate to impress the senior partner!

All of this may seem like a tall order. If you perform well on the first assignment, you can expect a rush of demand for more of these. It won't be long before the demand for your outlines and witness briefs morphs into the request for you to conduct the examinations yourself.

CONCLUSION

No cute bullet points to start this chapter. If you have read this far, you know the drill:

- Case analysis first.

- Figure out how to establish each of your elements.

- Attack each of theirs.

- Anticipate what could go wrong.

- Reduce risk.

- Settle your losers.

- Show up prepared.

The outline of any examination will reflect the author. A junior who works in tandem with a senior will add real value by applying the principles preached here.

MY ONE WAR STORY

At the golf club, a senior partner of a litigation boutique told me that his first year associate (my trainee) did a much better job preparing his examination outlines than he did. "And what about these 5-and-outs?" he asked. "They are fantastic." And that, to me, says it all.

CASE STUDY CASE SUMMARY

CASE SUMMARY

In this case, a young and inexperienced solicitor in a wills and estates boutique law firm makes contact with a wills client who is both elderly and in hospital. The solicitor meets with the client in the hospital, takes instructions to change the will, and awaits further instructions from the client. Three weeks later, the client dies of complications that arose in hospital.

The beneficiary named in the new will instructions starts a lawsuit for breach of duty by the solicitor.

LEGAL ENVIRONMENT

This is a matter of the common-law of negligence and contract. Legislation provides that a person is presumed to be capable unless proven otherwise. The common-law recognizes the duty of care that is owed by the solicitor to the beneficiaries who suffer a loss by reason of errors made in the drafting process. A holographic will is recognized by law. It is written only and entirely in the hand of the testator and signed. A codicil is a document that changes one (or more) of the terms of a will. Execution rules are the same as for wills.

CASE STUDY TIMELINE

1920 Birth of testator, Brian.

2013 January 15 Will prepared by Brian. Will names niece Carol as sole beneficiary. Will drafted by Lee, of Lee and Associates.

2014 December 1 Brian admitted into hospital. Diagnosed with terminal cancer and serious anemia, causing severe chest pains.

2014 December 15 Brian has Carol contact law firm by telephone. Arranges first meeting to review and change will.

2015 January 10 Brian has Carol contact law firm to arrange for meeting in hospital the next day.

2015 January 11 Kim attends at hospital to meet with Carol. Carol brings Kim to meet with Testator in the recovery room adjacent to the Emergency Department. Kim takes instructions to change the will.

2015 January 12 Kim meets with Lee to brief Lee on meeting with and instructions from Brian.

2015 January 21 Carol calls receptionist at law firm to advise that Brian plans to leave hospital on discharge and to meet at office to sign will. Requests date for appointment.

2015 January 28 Brian develops pneumonia as a complication from other illnesses. Brian becomes incapable.

2015 January 31 Brian dies from pneumonia.

2015 March 31 Another niece of Brian, Louise, retains legal counsel. Requests copy of file from Kim's firm.

2015 May 15 After negotiation and motion brought in court by lawyer for Louise, Lee and Associates provides a copy of the file to the lawyer for Louise, including the legible notes made by Kim that clearly show the instructions to change the will to include Louise as a 50% beneficiary.

2015 June 15 Louise commences lawsuit for damages against Kim and Lee and Associates for failing to act on the instructions from Brian.

LIST OF WITNESSES

Brian, testator and deceased

Carol and Lee are Brian's nieces.

Kim is a junior solicitor who works in the law offices of Lee and Associates.

Lee is founder and sole senior partner at Lee and Associates.

WITNESS STATEMENTS

STATEMENT OF CAROL

1. I am one of two sisters. Louise, and I are the only nieces of Brian. Our uncle had no nephews and no other nieces.

2. Brian and I were quite close throughout my adult life. Brian was very close to my three children, who treated him like a grandfather.

3. For some reason, Louise and Brian were not close.

4. Brian lived in an apartment not far from the offices of Lee and Associates.

5. Brian had a history of chest pain and other ailments, but was fairly healthy and independent until 2014. I know this because I took him to his medical appointments and filled his prescriptions at the local pharmacy.

6. I knew that he had drawn up a will in early 2014, but I did not know its contents.

7. In the summer of 2014, Brian suffered worse symptoms, especially in his chest. He increased his medications, including prescription morphine. He was able to speak with me as before, and I did not think him to be demented to any degree.

8. In late 2014, Brian was admitted to the City Hospital for pain in his chest. While there, the doctors diagnosed that he had serious cancer, from

which there was no recovery. He also suffered from severe anemia, which caused his chest pains.

9. While in the hospital, Brian's medications were increased. He had many sessions of severe sadness. I knew this because I visited with him several times a week. As a real estate agent, I have freedom to travel and visit with him as often as I liked.

10. I almost never saw Louise visit Brian at the hospital.

11. In the middle of December, Brian asked me to call Lee and Associates. He wanted to discuss his will.

12. I called the reception at Lee and Associates and arranged for an appointment. The appointment was to take place at their offices. I would drive Brian to and from either his apartment or the hospital.

13. Lee and Associates arranged a meeting at their offices for January 10 in the afternoon.

14. The morning of January 10, Brian was still in the hospital. I called Lee and Associates. I spoke with a lawyer there, named Kim. I arranged with Kim for a meeting in the hospital.

15. Kim arrived at 2 o'clock. I met with Kim in the lobby of the hospital. I said that it was very important that Brian sign a power of attorney because handling his financial affairs was becoming onerous.

16. I brought Kim to the second floor, to a room next to the Emergency Department where Brian had his

bed. There were three other patients in the rooms with beds surrounded by vertical drapes.

17. Brian asked me to run an errand for him, so I left. When I returned, Kim had already left.

18. Brian never told me what Kim and he had discussed.

19. 10 days later, or so, Brian told me that he was to be discharged from the hospital soon. He wanted me to contact Lee and Associates so that I could arrange for a meeting to sign his new will. He did not discuss the terms with me.

20. I called Lee and Associates. I asked for an appointment for Kim to meet with Brian. There was no appointment given, but I was told that I could drop in with a few hours notice.

21. January 28, Brian started to cough and hallucinate. He developed very serious illness, which I was told was pneumonia. Brian died of these complications within a few days. He was never lucid after he developed pneumonia.

22. In March, I told Louise that Brian had met with Kim and that the purpose was to make a new will.

23. Because I was the only beneficiary of the will, I instructed Lee and Associates to proceed through probate. After taxes and other expenses, I received the total value of the estate, $400,000.

Signed, *Carol*

STATEMENT OF LOUISE

1. I am one of the only two nieces of Brian.

2. Although Brian and I were never close, like Carol was, Brian and I talked and reconciled our differences.

3. I went to see him in the City Hospital several times after his admission in December 2014.

4. Carol seemed to stand guard over Brian, and was very protective of him. I visited when Louise was not around.

5. Brian and I were able to speak at length. He was always lucid.

6. He complained that Louise hovered over him and would not let him do what he wanted.

7. Brian told me in January that he expected to be discharged. He knew that he was very ill, but was told that he could stay at home, where he preferred to be.

8. Although Brian did not say this in so many words, he led me to believe that I would be named as an equal beneficiary with Carol in his will.

9. After he died in late January 2015, I asked Carol what the will said. I was shocked to learn that he did not make the changes that I believed he was making.

10. I retained legal counsel and inquired into what had been discussed between Lee and Associates and Brian in December and January.

11. That is why I brought this lawsuit. I believe that I am entitled to $200,000, or half the estate.

Signed, *Louise*

STATEMENT OF KIM

1. I am a junior associate, employed as such with the law firm of Lee and Associates. I have worked at this firm since summer 2014. I was called to the Bar of this jurisdiction in June 2014.

2. I did not have any formal training in a solicitors practice of wills and estates, although I took the course in law school.

3. When I arrived at Lee and associates, Lee told me that we would work together on files until I was reasonably confident that I could take instructions directly.

4. Over the course of the next few months, I worked with Lee on wills files as well as powers of attorney. I helped the staff probate Estates.

5. In December 2014, I was contacted by the receptionist at the firm. Carol had called to request an appointment.

6. I pulled the old will file for Brian, and saw that this was a typical and customary will. Brian's niece,

Carol, was executor and sole beneficiary. There was no mention of anybody else in the family.

7. The receptionist made an appointment for January 10, take place at our offices. I was not told that Brian was in the hospital.

8. The morning of January 10, the receptionist put a call through to me from Carol. I was told that Brian was in the hospital, as he had been since December. Carol and I agreed that I was to go to the hospital and meet with Carol who would introduce me to Brian.

9. This was the first occasion when I was to meet a client outside the office. I had never met a client in the hospital.

10. At this point, I had never taken instructions directly from a client to make a new will. However, I did know how to test for capacity and how to take instructions.

11. The next afternoon, I met with Carol in the lobby of the hospital. I was told that Brian should prepare a power of attorney, as Carol had to look after Brian's financial affairs. This was very difficult without having the formal power. I said that I would take Brian's instructions.

12. I met with Brian in the hospital overflow room adjacent to the Emergency Department. Brian was clearly very old and was quite sick. There were patients nearby in bed, so I did not feel that we have much privacy.

13. Brian was sitting up in bed, and had a table beside his bed. Brian ask Carol to go to the pharmacy and pick up razor blades or something like that.

14. After Carroll left, Brian told me that he wanted to change his will. He felt badly about how he had left his other niece, Louise, out of his will. He wanted to include her as a 50% beneficiary.

15. I could not ask the normal questions about capacity that I knew were necessary. Just was because there was no privacy. Brian told me that he wanted to sign the will when he was discharged from hospital, which she expected fairly soon.

16. I asked Brian whether he wanted me to prepare a power of attorney. I expressed what Carroll had told me Brian said he felt quite capable of looking after his own affairs. He did not want Carol to "meddle", to use his word.

17. The whole meeting took less than 20 minutes. I did not take notes at that time, because there was not much need for this.

18. When I returned to the office, I immediately made notes of the meeting with Brian. These notes are attached as Exhibit One.

19. The next day, I asked to see Lee. We met for less than half an hour, about this and other subjects. I told Lee about the meeting.

20. I specifically asked Lee about the power of attorney. Lee told me that I should take the client's direction. If the client does not want a power of attorney, I was not to do one.

21. Lee asked me if I needed help with the will. I said there was no rush. I would ask Lee if I needed help at the time that I drafted it.

22. Because this was a garden-variety simple Will, I felt that I could do it when the time was made for an appointment to sign it.

23. I was called on January 21. Carol had called reception to ask for an appointment for us to meet with Brian. There was no urgency communicated to me.

24. The next I heard was in early February that Brian had passed away from complications of pneumonia.

Signed, *Kim*

STATEMENT OF LEE

1. I am a lawyer who practices in the field of wills and Estates. Before I became a lawyer, I was a qualified and practicing nurse.

2. I founded Lee and Associates in 2001. From the outset, this firm has specialized in wills and Estates practice.

3. I have had other associates from time to time. At any one time, I only have one associate. I have several law clerks who assist in dealing with clients and arranging for appointments, passing probate and accounts.

4. Early 2013, I prepared a will for Brian. He had not been a client earlier. The will was a simple one,

naming his niece, Carol, as executor and sole beneficiary.

5. There was nothing unusual about the will. There was no mention of other members of the family. I cannot recall discussing the case with Brian. Although I made notes at the time, It has been my practice to have these notes shredded within six months of closing the file, which was 2013.

6. In summer 2014, I decided to hire a young associate, Kim. Kim came well recommended and had good marks from law school. I knew that Kim did not have any experience with wills and Estates. This was fine with me, because I like to train the associates in the way that I conduct practice.

7. In December 2014, our receptionist received a telephone call from Carol on behalf of Brian. It seems that Brian wanted to change the terms of his will. No details were provided by telephone.

8. Because this was shortly before Christmas, we arranged for Brian to come to see us on January 11, 2015.

9. Apparently, Carol called to change the arrangements for a hospital visit. I had no trouble with Kim going to the hospital to see Brian. This was going to be a simple will, after all.

10. On January 12, I met with Kim about Brian and other subjects. The only concern that Kim had was whether to force a power of attorney upon Brian. I said not to do this, as Kim well understood without my guidance. Nothing else came up about Brian's

case. I offered to help, but thought that this was a good opportunity for Kim to do the work alone.

11. I learned afterwards that Carol called our receptionist on January 21 to ask for another appointment for Brian to sign the will.

12. The next that we heard was that Brian passed away at the end of January.

13. Carol was the only executor. We contacted Carol and arranged to prepare probate. We handled the estate, which amounted to just over $400,000 net of income tax and other charges. We wrote a trust cheque to Carol for the entire balance.

14. When Louise contacted us through her lawyer, we consulted the Bar. We were told to cooperate. After a motion was brought for an order for us to turn over the file notes, we did so under direction of the Bar.

Signed, *Lee*

CASE STUDY EXHIBITS

EXHIBIT 1 – HANDWRITTEN NOTES OF KIM, DATED JANUARY 11, 2015

Met with Brian, a former client of Lee. Wants to change will to include second niece, Louise. Discussed reasons, and said reconciliation, felt bad about earlier disposition, unhappy with Carol, who is very bossy and controlling.

Brian advised that he will get out of hospital sooner or later. Wants to sign will at the office.

I raised power of attorney, as requested by Carol. Brian wants no part of this. Carol meddles too much as it is. He can look after himself, he says.

Did not deal with nature of estate, and moral obligations. Have no qualms about capacity, however. No privacy in the overflow room where Brian is staying. Will deal with capacity at next visit.

Direction from Brian to sign will in our office when he is discharged. Does not want Carol involved.

Signed, *Kim*

EXHIBIT 2 – HOSPITAL RECORDS OF CITY HOSPITAL

July 5, 2014 Brian attends as outpatient, test for anemia and suspected cancer. Blood tests conducted.

July 12, 2014 Brian attends as outpatient. Review of test results. Very severe anemia. Clear and proven cancer with melanoma spread through lymph system. Inoperable. Discussed treatment options, but Brian rejected chemotherapy and Radiology treatments. DNR instructions. Referral to social worker in house.

July 19, 2014 Brian attends as outpatient with his niece, Carol, to consult social worker. After review, he is reliant upon niece, Carol. He is able to live independently so long as Carol make sure he takes his medication and sees him once a day at least for ordinary care. A visit by home care nurse every second day is advisable. Brian gives instructions and is clearly capable of making decisions.

December 1, 2014 Brian is brought to hospital in ambulance. Complains of chest pain and pain throughout body. Consistent with summer diagnosis of anemia and cancer. Recommend palliative care and increased medications. Is brought to overflow room at emergency department because City Hospital capacity is overloaded with patients.

December 2 to January 28, 2014 list of medications, including sleeping medications, pain medications, and Anemia treatment. List of hospital visits by visitors shows daily visits by Carol, and visits by Louise three times a week. Never when Carol is present. Shows visit by Kim on afternoon January 11, 2015

January 28 2015 chart shows onset of pneumonia, deterioration and death January 31, 2015. Autopsy confirmed diagnosis from summer 2014.

EXHIBIT 3 – SUMMARY OF LAST WILL AND TESTAMENT OF BRIAN, DATED JANUARY 2013

1. Appoints Carol, niece, as sole executor.

2. Leaves residue of estate to Carol.

3. Should Carol predecease, residue left to named charities.

CASE STUDY PLEADINGS

Louise, Plaintiff

And

Lee and Associates and Kim, Defendants

Statement of Claim

1. The plaintiff claims from the defendants damages of
    $200,000, interest and costs.

2. The plaintiff resides in the City and is the niece of
    Brian, who died January 31, 2015 in the City
    Hospital.

3. The defendants are respectively a law firm and a
    lawyer who conduct their law practice in the City.

4. Brian retained the defendants to draft a will to name
    the plaintiff as a beneficiary.

5. The defendants failed to complete their mandate
    within a reasonable time, knowing that Brian was at
    risk of early mortality.

6. Brian died, leaving Louise no gift from his estate.

7. The defendants owed to Brian and to Louise the
    duty to comply with Brian's direction in a timely
    manner, which duty they breached. The breach of
    duty caused Louise damages of $200,000.

Dated at the City, June 15, 2015.

Louise, Plaintiff

And

Lee and Associates and Kim, Defendants

Statement of Defence

1. The defendants deny the retainer as alleged in the Statement of Claim.

2. Brian asked to consult the defendants with respect to a will. He specifically directed the defendants to await his discharge from City Hospital.

3. Brian died before his discharge and without changing his directions to the defendants.

4. Brian chose to act through his niece, Carol, who stood to suffer a loss should the will be executed as pleaded by Louise. If anyone caused a loss to the plaintiff, the responsible party is Carol, not the defendants.

5. The defendants owed neither a duty to Brian nor to the plaintiff. The defendants breached no such duty.

6. The plaintiffs acted reasonably and on directions from their client, who was Brian throughout.

Dated at the City, July 30, 2015.

---

[1] **Odgers on High Court Pleading and** Practice (23rd ed.), D. B. Casson (Sweet & Maxwell)

www.ingramcontent.com/pod-product-compliance
Lightning Source LLC
Chambersburg PA
CBHW060614210326
41520CB00010B/1336